D1600485

Salaam: Mindfulness for Muslims

Written by: Humera Malik
Illustrated by: Najwa Awatiff

© Green Key Press 2021

A publication of:
Green Key Press
Washington, DC

For further information, please visit greenkeypress.com.

ISBN 978-0-9989-782-5-3
10 9 8 7 6 5 4 3 2 1

⚷
**GREEN KEY
PRESS**

SALAAM:

MINDFULNESS FOR MUSLIMS

Also by the Author

The Story of the Holy Prophet Muhammad,
peace and blessings of Allah be on him

Is My Mom Like Other Moms?

Be Sure to Pray, Zain!

Contents

Note for Parents

Mindfulness is the practice of acknowledging our feelings with kindness. Emotional intelligence is the ability to manage those emotions in a positive way. These skills will help children deal with adversity, foster better relationships, perform better in school, and be more content and optimistic in life.

Keeping Allah at the forefront of a child's emotional education strengthens a child's faith and helps relieve anxiety. The Qur'an, Sunnah, and Hadith provide us with every tool needed to handle a myriad of emotions, from uplifting motivation to affirmations and actionable items. This book is designed to be read from cover to cover in peaceful times and to be dipped into to find specific advice when handling a particular emotion. For each emotion, children are provided with three kinds of coping mechanisms:

"Remember" - An inspirational verse of the Holy Qur'an to remind children of the love that Allah has for them.

"Say" - An affirmation in the form of a Qur'anic verse, du'a, or dhikr which has a calming effect on the mind, heart, and body when repeated.

"Do" - Simple activities that children can do, in the given moment or over time, to help them develop self-regulating skills.

Children will eventually learn these motivational verses, affirmations, and activities by heart and be able to draw on them when handling difficult emotions. All the verses and activities bring children back to Allah and enjoin Islamic practices. These pages are packed with important Qur'anic verses and ahadith and every time your child picks up this book, a different verse, activity, or hadith will jump out at them, making the act of reading this book a unique experience every time, inshallah.

i

Note for Young Readers

It is normal for our hearts to feel big emotions! But did you know that Allah does not want us to despair of His mercy? Allah has given us all the things we need to feel better. There are prayers we can say and actions we can do. Sometimes we need to cry and sometimes we have to apologize. At other times we just need to breathe and be quiet.

So when you feel any of the emotions listed in the Contents, pick up this book for guidance. It will remind you of how much Allah loves you and help you to start feeling better. Remember, no matter how big your feelings are, Allah is bigger and stronger and He is always with you.

Your friend,
Humera

Afraid

As for those who say,
"our Lord is Allah"
and then remain steadfast,
the angels descend on them,
saying, "Fear ye not, nor grieve."

(41:30)

Say:

لَا حَوْلَ وَلَا قُوَّةَ إِلَّا بِاللهِ

Lā ḥaula wa lā quwwata illā billāh

There is neither power nor any might except with Allah.

(Ibn Majah)

When I feel Afraid I can...

Checklist:
- ☑ Do a good deed
- ☑ Give in charity
- ☑ Recite last three Surahs

1 Do a good deed. Even a smile counts!

Do not belittle any **GOOD DEED**, even meeting your brother with a **CHEERFUL FACE**

MUSLIM

2 Give in charity. Provide food for someone who is hungry.

Angry

Remember:

Strong is the one
who can control
his anger.

(Bukhari)

Say:

أَعُوذُ بِاللهِ مِنَ الشَيْطَانِ الرَّجِيْم

A'ūdhu billāhi minash-shayṭānir-rajīm

I seek refuge with Allah from Satan the Accursed.

(41:36)

When I feel Angry I can...

Checklist:
- ☑ Stop
- ☑ Stay quiet
- ☑ Sit or lie down
- ☑ Do ablution

2 Stay quiet.
Take calming breaths

Speak A GOOD WORD or REMAIN Silent

Bukhari

1 Stop.
Try counting to 5.

STOP

WHEN THEY GET Angry THEY forgive
42:37

3 Sit or lie down.

4 Do ablution with cool water.

Disappointed

And it may be that you dislike a thing which is good for you and that you like a thing which is bad for you. **Allah knows** but you do not know.

(4:19)

Say:

وَاللّٰهُ خَيْرُ الْمَاكِرِيْن

Wallāhu khayrul-mākirīn

Allah is the
Best of Planners.

15

(3:54)

When I feel Disappointed I can...

Checklist:

- ☑ Count my blessings
- ☑ Trust Allah
- ☑ Be grateful

1

Count my blessings.
I can say 5 things I am thankful for.

Be THANKFUL to GOD
31:12

5 THINGS
i am thankful for...

1.
2.
3.
4.
5.

2 Put my trust in Allah.

Tawakkul

Whoever **puts** all his **TRUST** in **ALLAH**, He will be **ENOUGH** for him
65:3

Whoever is **GRATEFUL** I will **Give** him **more**
14:7

Shukr

 3 Accept with gratitude what I receive.

Grief

Remember:

Surely there is **ease**

after hardship.

(94:5)

Say:

إِنَّا لِلّهِ وَإِنَّا إِلَيْهِ رَاجِعُوْن

Innā lillāhi wa innā ilayhi rāji'ūn

Truly, to Allah we belong and truly, to Him we shall return.

(2:156)

When I feel Grief I can...

CHECKLIST:
- ☑ Cry
- ☑ Use calm words
- ☑ Turn to Allah

1 Cry before Allah.

2 Avoid using angry words or raising my voice.

We do not say anything except that which pleases Allah

muslim

STRONG

BE KIND

I can

3 Turn to Allah for comfort.

Surely in the REMEMBRANCE of ALLAH do Hearts Find Comfort - 13:28

Jealous

Remember:

Thy Lord **does not wrong** anyone.

(18:49)

Say:

رَبِّ أَوْزِعْنِيْ أَنْ أَشْكُرَ نِعْمَتَكَ الَّتِيْ أَنْعَمْتَ عَلَيَّ

Rabbi auzi'nī an ashkura ni'matakallatī an'amta 'allayya

My Lord! Grant me the will and power to be grateful for Your favor which You have bestowed upon me.

27

(27:19)

When I feel Jealous I can...

CheCkLiSt:

- ☑ Count my blessings
- ☑ Stop the comparisons
- ☑ Seek refuge in Allah

1 Be thankful for what you do have.

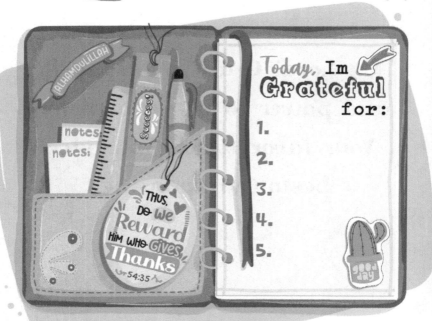

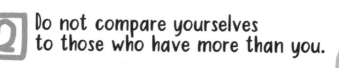

2 Do not compare yourselves to those who have more than you.

Jealous

IF you are Grateful, I will surely Increase you [in Favor] 14:7

Count your blessings, say Alhamdulillah

3 Seek refuge in Allah from envy.

Lonely

Allah is the **Friend** of those who believe. He brings them out of every kind of darkness into light.

(2:257)

Say:

وَكَفَىٰ بِاللّٰهِ وَلِيًّا

Wa kafā billāhi waliyyan

Sufficient is Allah as a Friend.

(4:45)

When I feel Lonely I can...

ChecKLiSt:

- ☑ Greet others with Salaam
- ☑ Pray in congregation at home / local mosque
- ☑ Ask a friend, 'How are you?'
- ☑ Make someone feel special

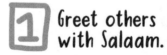

1 Greet others with Salaam.

2 Pray in congregation at masjid or home.

Lonely

3

Ask a friend,
'How are you?'

BFF

ME — SaLaam! How are you doing?

BFF — WassaLam! FeeLing great! How about you?

ME — I'm good.. THanK you For asKing.. :)

BFF — THat's Great! want to come over?

4 Make someone feel special.

thank you!

Overwhelmed

Remember:

Allah burdens not any **soul**

beyond its capacity.

(65:7)

Say:

أَنِّي مَغْلُوْبٌ فَانْتَصِرْ

Annī maghlūbun fantaṣir

I am overcome,
so come Ye to my help!

(54:10)

When I feel Overwhelmed I can...

Checklist:
- ☑ Pray
- ☑ Plan
- ☑ Prioritize salaat

1 Start with a prayer.

seek **help** with **PATIENCE** and **PRAYER** 2:45

2 Make a step-by-step plan.

Daily Plan

SCHEDULE

Fajr

Dhuhr

Asr

Maghrib

Isha

GUARD STRICTLY YOUR HABIT OF PRAYER

2:238

Salaat tracker

S M T W T F S

NOTES:
....
....
....

WELL DONE!

PLANNER

3 Plan my day around the five daily prayers.

Sad

It is in the remembrance of Allah that **hearts** can find comfort.

(13:28)

Say:

حَسْبِيَ اللّٰهُ لَا إِلَاهَ إِلَّا هُوَ۔

عَلَيْهِ تَوَكَّلْتُ وَهُوَ رَبُّ الْعَرْشِ الْعَظِيْمِ

Ḥasbiyallāhu lā ilāha illāhū.

'Alayhi tawakkaltu wa huwa Rabbul 'arshil 'aẓīm.

Allah is sufficient for me. There is no god but He. In Him do I put my trust, and He is the Lord of the mighty Throne.

45

(9:128)

When I feel Sad I can...

Checklist:
- ☑ Remember Allah
- ☑ Recite the Quran
- ☑ Call upon Him by His Names

1 Remember Allah in prayer.

2 Recite the Quran.

DO NOT BE SAD, INDEED Allah IS WITH US

9:40

Shy

Nothing shall befall us save that which Allah has ordained for us. He is **our Protector.** And in Allah then should the believers put their trust.

(9:50)

Say:

رَبِّ اشْرَحْ لِيْ صَدْرِيْ وَيَسِّرْ لِيْ أَمْرِيْ وَاحْلُلْ عُقْدَةً مِّنْ لِّسَانِيْ يَفْقَهُوْا قَوْلِيْ

Rabbishraḥ lī ṣadrī wa yassir lī amrī waḥlul

'uqdatam-mil-lisānī yafqahū qaulī.

O my Lord! Open for me my chest and ease my task for me and loosen the knot from my tongue, that they understand my speech.

51

(20:25-28)

When I feel Shy I can...

CheCKLiSt:

- ☑ Remember Allah is the Protector
- ☑ Be prepared
- ☑ Say a Prayer

1 Remind myself that Allah is my Protector.

But Allah is your Protector and He is the **Best of Helpers** 3:150

2 Practice and be prepared.

My Lord, Grant me Courage ~20:25~

I am BRAVE

Sorry

Surely **Allah forgives** all sins. Verily, He is Most Forgiving, Merciful.

(39:53)

Say:

اَللّٰهُمَّ إِنَّكَ عُفُوٌّ كَرِيْمٌ تُحِبُّ الْعَفْوَ فَاعْفُ عَنِّيْ

Allāhumma innaka ʿufuwwun karīmun
tuḥibbul ʿafwa faʿfu ʿannī

Oh Allah! You are the Benevolent Forgiver, you love forgiving, so forgive me!

57

(Tirmidhi)

When I feel Sorry I can...

ChECKLiSt:
- ☑ Apologize
- ☑ Seek forgiveness
- ☑ Give to charity
- ☑ Do a good deed

1 Apologize.

I'm Sorry!

2 Seek Allah's forgiveness.

The Absolute Forgiver

3 Give charity.

CHARITY

Sorry

4 Do a good deed.

Surely, Good Deeds erase Bad Deeds
11:114

Upset

Remember:

Pray unto Me,

I will answer your prayer.

(40:60)

Say:

رَبِّ إِنِّي لِمَآ أَنْزَلْتَ إِلَيَّ مِنْ خَيْرٍ فَقِيرٌ

Rabbi innī limā anzalta ilayya min khayrin faqīr

My Lord! I am in need of whatever good You may send down to me.

63

(28:24)

When I feel Upset I can...

CheckList:
- ☑ Pray
- ☑ Seek comfort in Allah
- ☑ Remember- I am strong!

1 Pray in prostration to Allah.

PROSTRATE & draw near ►[TO ALLAH]◄ 96:19

2 Seek Comfort in Allah.

Quran

Allah's Names

Dhikr

3 Remind myself that I am strong enough to handle this.

Be STRONG
Be FOCUSED
beat the rest

WORK HARD

Allah does not burden a SOUL BEYOND its capacity
2:286

I CAN DO IT

Be Positive

Worried

The one who puts his **trust in Allah,** He is sufficient for him.

(65:3)

Say:

حَسْبُنَا اللّٰهُ وَنِعْمَ الْوَكِيْل

Ḥasbunallāhu wa niʿmal-wakīl

Sufficient for us is Allah and an excellent Guardian is He.

(3:173)

69

When I feel Worried I can...

Checklist:
- ✅ Remember Allah is in control
- ✅ Pray
- ✅ Put my trust in Allah
- ✅ Tie my camel

1 Remember Allah is in control.

ALLAH is the **best** of PLANNERS 8:30

2 Pray in the last third of the night.

WHO WILL ask of me that I may **answer** BuKHari

3 Put my trust in Allah.

Trust in ALLAH but Tie your camel

Tirmidhi

4 Tie my camel
by trying my best.

Grateful

Remember:

If you are **grateful,**

I will, surely, bestow more favors

on you.

(14:7)

Say:

سُبْحَانَ اللهِ وَالْحَمْدُ لِلّهِ وَلَا إِلَاهَ إِلَّا اللهُ وَاللهُ أَكْبَرُ

Subḥānallāhi walḥamdu lillāhi

wa lā ilāha illallāhu wallāhu akbar

Holy is Allah and all praise
belongs to Allah and there is
no god besides Allah and
Allah is the greatest.

(Muslim)

When I feel Grateful I can...

1 Give thanks with my heart by offering nafl prayer.

"WHoever PRAYS (tHe OPTioNAL) 12 raka'ah in a day and night, a HOUSE wiLL be buiLt For Him in JANNAH"

MusLim

2 Give thanks with words by praising Allah.

ALL praise is For Allah—LORD OF aLL worLds 1:2

ALHAMDULILLAH

3 Give thanks with my actions by doing a good deed.

Grateful